# 3RD GRADE MIX TWO-DIGIT VERTICAL MULTIPLICATION AND DIVISION WORKBOOK

## CHILDREN'S MATH BOOKS

**BABY PROFESSOR**

EDUCATION KIDS

Speedy Publishing LLC

40 E. Main St. #1156

Newark, DE 19711

www.speedypublishing.com

Copyright 2016

Practice multiplication and division with this workbook. This will help you love math even more.

Have Fun Learning Kid!

# MULTIPLICATION EXERCISES

**Find the product.**

# MULTIPLICATION

Name: ........................................................................................................

Date: ..............................................................  Score: ...............................

1.)  90
  x  33

2.)  67
  x  57

3.)  48
  x  83

4.)  67
  x  70

5.)  79
  x  67

6.)  64
  x  76

7.)  16
  x  21

8.)  63
  x  82

Name: .....................................................................................

Date: ..............................................................   Score: ...........................................

1.]
$$\begin{array}{r} 89 \\ \times \ 62 \\ \hline \end{array}$$

2.]
$$\begin{array}{r} 39 \\ \times \ 59 \\ \hline \end{array}$$

3.]
$$\begin{array}{r} 66 \\ \times \ 58 \\ \hline \end{array}$$

4.]
$$\begin{array}{r} 20 \\ \times \ 45 \\ \hline \end{array}$$

5.]
$$\begin{array}{r} 64 \\ \times \ 91 \\ \hline \end{array}$$

6.]
$$\begin{array}{r} 32 \\ \times \ 27 \\ \hline \end{array}$$

7.]
$$\begin{array}{r} 12 \\ \times \ 17 \\ \hline \end{array}$$

8.]
$$\begin{array}{r} 73 \\ \times \ 19 \\ \hline \end{array}$$

Name: ...............................................................................................

Date: .................................................................   Score: ...........................

1.]  98
   x 60

2.]  16
   x 56

3.]  41
   x 37

4.]  10
   x 54

5.]  34
   x 14

6.]  16
   x 89

7.]  59
   x 34

8.]  36
   x 96

Name: ........................................................................

Date: ........................................................................    Score: ........................................

1.]    24
    x  64

2.]    44
    x  23

3.]    25
    x  33

4.]    34
    x  45

5.]    52
    x  31

6.]    21
    x  66

7.]    50
    x  83

8.]    60
    x  79

Name: ...............................................................................................................

Date: ..................................................................... Score: .................................

1.]
$$\begin{array}{r} 92 \\ \times\ 61 \\ \hline \end{array}$$

2.]
$$\begin{array}{r} 45 \\ \times\ 58 \\ \hline \end{array}$$

3.]
$$\begin{array}{r} 33 \\ \times\ 61 \\ \hline \end{array}$$

4.]
$$\begin{array}{r} 64 \\ \times\ 70 \\ \hline \end{array}$$

5.]
$$\begin{array}{r} 58 \\ \times\ 64 \\ \hline \end{array}$$

6.]
$$\begin{array}{r} 94 \\ \times\ 12 \\ \hline \end{array}$$

7.]
$$\begin{array}{r} 34 \\ \times\ 88 \\ \hline \end{array}$$

8.]
$$\begin{array}{r} 13 \\ \times\ 80 \\ \hline \end{array}$$

Name: .............................................................................................................

Date: .................................................................... Score: ....................................

1.]
```
     13
x    48
```

2.]
```
     54
x    76
```

3.]
```
     80
x    30
```

4.]
```
     11
x    24
```

5.]
```
     76
x    32
```

6.]
```
     57
x    20
```

7.]
```
     41
x    75
```

8.]
```
     66
x    60
```

Name: ...................................................................................................

Date: .................................................................. Score: ....................................

1.]
```
    69
x   24
_____
```

2.]
```
    88
x   54
_____
```

3.]
```
    56
x   98
_____
```

4.]
```
    91
x   16
_____
```

5.]
```
    39
x   60
_____
```

6.]
```
    16
x   86
_____
```

7.]
```
    40
x   68
_____
```

8.]
```
    40
x   89
_____
```

Name: ...................................................................................................

Date: ..................................................................................  Score: .................................

1.]
$$\begin{array}{r} 96 \\ \times\ 76 \\ \hline \end{array}$$

2.]
$$\begin{array}{r} 78 \\ \times\ 20 \\ \hline \end{array}$$

3.]
$$\begin{array}{r} 38 \\ \times\ 36 \\ \hline \end{array}$$

4.]
$$\begin{array}{r} 15 \\ \times\ 71 \\ \hline \end{array}$$

5.]
$$\begin{array}{r} 35 \\ \times\ 84 \\ \hline \end{array}$$

6.]
$$\begin{array}{r} 35 \\ \times\ 12 \\ \hline \end{array}$$

7.]
$$\begin{array}{r} 33 \\ \times\ 19 \\ \hline \end{array}$$

8.]
$$\begin{array}{r} 27 \\ \times\ 35 \\ \hline \end{array}$$

# MULTIPLICATION

Name: ......................................................................................................

Date: ....................................................................... Score: ...............................

1.)
$$\begin{array}{r} 59 \\ \times\ 70 \\ \hline \end{array}$$

2.)
$$\begin{array}{r} 21 \\ \times\ 77 \\ \hline \end{array}$$

3.)
$$\begin{array}{r} 95 \\ \times\ 92 \\ \hline \end{array}$$

4.)
$$\begin{array}{r} 33 \\ \times\ 78 \\ \hline \end{array}$$

5.)
$$\begin{array}{r} 25 \\ \times\ 52 \\ \hline \end{array}$$

6.)
$$\begin{array}{r} 33 \\ \times\ 56 \\ \hline \end{array}$$

7.)
$$\begin{array}{r} 83 \\ \times\ 19 \\ \hline \end{array}$$

8.)
$$\begin{array}{r} 73 \\ \times\ 13 \\ \hline \end{array}$$

Name: ........................................................................................

Date: ................................................................ Score: ..........................

1.)
```
    42
x   17
-------
   714
```

2.)
```
    72
x   57
-------
  4104
```

3.)
```
    37
x   47
-------
  1739
```

4.)
```
    62
x   27
-------
  1674
```

5.)
```
    38
x   28
-------
  1064
```

6.)
```
    67
x   41
-------
  2747
```

7.)
```
    24
x   36
-------
   864
```

8.)
```
    72
x   48
-------
  3456
```

Name: .............................................................................................................................

Date: ...........................................................................  Score: ....................................

1.]
```
    18
x   19
_____
```

2.]
```
    50
x   25
_____
```

3.]
```
    27
x   12
_____
```

4.]
```
    66
x   44
_____
```

5.]
```
    61
x   21
_____
```

6.]
```
    87
x   11
_____
```

7.]
```
    22
x   22
_____
```

8.]
```
    84
x   33
_____
```

Name: ...........................................................................................................

Date: ...............................................................   Score: ...........................................

1.]
$$\begin{array}{r} 91 \\ \times\ 95 \\ \hline \end{array}$$

2.]
$$\begin{array}{r} 16 \\ \times\ 73 \\ \hline \end{array}$$

3.]
$$\begin{array}{r} 95 \\ \times\ 40 \\ \hline \end{array}$$

4.]
$$\begin{array}{r} 52 \\ \times\ 50 \\ \hline \end{array}$$

5.]
$$\begin{array}{r} 27 \\ \times\ 21 \\ \hline \end{array}$$

6.]
$$\begin{array}{r} 45 \\ \times\ 84 \\ \hline \end{array}$$

7.]
$$\begin{array}{r} 28 \\ \times\ 53 \\ \hline \end{array}$$

8.]
$$\begin{array}{r} 56 \\ \times\ 10 \\ \hline \end{array}$$

# MULTIPLICATION

Name: ................................................................

Date: ..............................................    Score: ...........................

1.)  $\begin{array}{r} 10 \\ \times\ 40 \\ \hline \end{array}$

2.)  $\begin{array}{r} 86 \\ \times\ 38 \\ \hline \end{array}$

3.)  $\begin{array}{r} 83 \\ \times\ 25 \\ \hline \end{array}$

4.)  $\begin{array}{r} 33 \\ \times\ 40 \\ \hline \end{array}$

5.)  $\begin{array}{r} 44 \\ \times\ 31 \\ \hline \end{array}$

6.)  $\begin{array}{r} 24 \\ \times\ 85 \\ \hline \end{array}$

7.)  $\begin{array}{r} 64 \\ \times\ 47 \\ \hline \end{array}$

8.)  $\begin{array}{r} 46 \\ \times\ 65 \\ \hline \end{array}$

Name: ......................................................................

Date: ..........................................  Score: ................................

1.]  88
  x 79

2.]  80
  x 40

3.]  15
  x 47

4.]  78
  x 54

5.]  78
  x 62

6.]  61
  x 33

7.]  33
  x 46

8.]  72
  x 15

# MULTIPLICATION

Name: ...........................................................................................

Date: .........................................................  Score: ...........................................

1.)
$$\begin{array}{r} 21 \\ \times\ 40 \\ \hline \end{array}$$

2.)
$$\begin{array}{r} 66 \\ \times\ 89 \\ \hline \end{array}$$

3.)
$$\begin{array}{r} 56 \\ \times\ 14 \\ \hline \end{array}$$

4.)
$$\begin{array}{r} 11 \\ \times\ 92 \\ \hline \end{array}$$

5.)
$$\begin{array}{r} 23 \\ \times\ 16 \\ \hline \end{array}$$

6.)
$$\begin{array}{r} 17 \\ \times\ 62 \\ \hline \end{array}$$

7.)
$$\begin{array}{r} 19 \\ \times\ 31 \\ \hline \end{array}$$

8.)
$$\begin{array}{r} 82 \\ \times\ 88 \\ \hline \end{array}$$

Name: ..................................................................................................

Date: ........................................................... Score: ................................

1.]  $\begin{array}{r} 50 \\ \times\ 28 \\ \hline \end{array}$

2.]  $\begin{array}{r} 47 \\ \times\ 77 \\ \hline \end{array}$

3.]  $\begin{array}{r} 93 \\ \times\ 65 \\ \hline \end{array}$

4.]  $\begin{array}{r} 34 \\ \times\ 75 \\ \hline \end{array}$

5.]  $\begin{array}{r} 99 \\ \times\ 53 \\ \hline \end{array}$

6.]  $\begin{array}{r} 55 \\ \times\ 63 \\ \hline \end{array}$

7.]  $\begin{array}{r} 58 \\ \times\ 71 \\ \hline \end{array}$

8.]  $\begin{array}{r} 53 \\ \times\ 79 \\ \hline \end{array}$

# MULTIPLICATION

Name: .........................................................................................................

Date: .......................................................................... Score: ...........................

1.)
$$\begin{array}{r} 21 \\ \times\ 40 \\ \hline \end{array}$$

2.)
$$\begin{array}{r} 66 \\ \times\ 89 \\ \hline \end{array}$$

3.)
$$\begin{array}{r} 56 \\ \times\ 14 \\ \hline \end{array}$$

4.)
$$\begin{array}{r} 11 \\ \times\ 92 \\ \hline \end{array}$$

5.)
$$\begin{array}{r} 23 \\ \times\ 16 \\ \hline \end{array}$$

6.)
$$\begin{array}{r} 17 \\ \times\ 62 \\ \hline \end{array}$$

7.)
$$\begin{array}{r} 19 \\ \times\ 31 \\ \hline \end{array}$$

8.)
$$\begin{array}{r} 82 \\ \times\ 88 \\ \hline \end{array}$$

Name: ..............................................................................................................

Date: ..................................................................... Score: ...........................................

1.]
$$50 \times 28$$

2.]
$$47 \times 77$$

3.]
$$93 \times 65$$

4.]
$$34 \times 75$$

5.]
$$99 \times 53$$

6.]
$$55 \times 63$$

7.]
$$58 \times 71$$

8.]
$$53 \times 79$$

# MULTIPLICATION

Name: ...........................................................................................................

Date: .................................................................................... Score: ............................................

1.)
$$\begin{array}{r} 48 \\ \times\ 29 \\ \hline \end{array}$$

2.)
$$\begin{array}{r} 25 \\ \times\ 43 \\ \hline \end{array}$$

3.)
$$\begin{array}{r} 89 \\ \times\ 13 \\ \hline \end{array}$$

4.)
$$\begin{array}{r} 59 \\ \times\ 71 \\ \hline \end{array}$$

5.)
$$\begin{array}{r} 11 \\ \times\ 21 \\ \hline \end{array}$$

6.)
$$\begin{array}{r} 83 \\ \times\ 85 \\ \hline \end{array}$$

7.)
$$\begin{array}{r} 42 \\ \times\ 96 \\ \hline \end{array}$$

8.)
$$\begin{array}{r} 66 \\ \times\ 10 \\ \hline \end{array}$$

# MULTIPLICATION

Name: ...........................................................................................

Date: ..................................................... Score: ...............................

1.]
$$\begin{array}{r} 42 \\ \times\ 50 \\ \hline \end{array}$$

2.]
$$\begin{array}{r} 91 \\ \times\ 90 \\ \hline \end{array}$$

3.]
$$\begin{array}{r} 89 \\ \times\ 75 \\ \hline \end{array}$$

4.]
$$\begin{array}{r} 24 \\ \times\ 91 \\ \hline \end{array}$$

5.]
$$\begin{array}{r} 81 \\ \times\ 26 \\ \hline \end{array}$$

6.]
$$\begin{array}{r} 25 \\ \times\ 88 \\ \hline \end{array}$$

7.]
$$\begin{array}{r} 21 \\ \times\ 88 \\ \hline \end{array}$$

8.]
$$\begin{array}{r} 18 \\ \times\ 93 \\ \hline \end{array}$$

# DIVISION EXERCISES

**Find the quotient.**

Name: .......................................................................................................

Date: .............................................................................. Score: ...........................................

1.] $24\overline{)144}$

2.] $72\overline{)396}$

3.] $46\overline{)1886}$

4.] $48\overline{)4668}$

5.] $12\overline{)78}$

6.] $42\overline{)693}$

Name: .................................................................................................

Date: .................................................................    Score: ...............................

---

**1.)** $21\overline{)126}$

**2.)** $24\overline{)1326}$

**3.)** $47\overline{)1598}$

**4.)** $35\overline{)3430}$

**5.)** $13\overline{)26}$

**6.)** $45\overline{)1719}$

## DIVISION

Name: .......................................................................................................

Date: .......................................................................   Score: ..............................

1.] $32\overline{)48}$

2.] $15\overline{)528}$

3.] $64\overline{)272}$

4.] $68\overline{)5321}$

5.] $37\overline{)1554}$

6.] $42\overline{)4032}$

Name: ......................................................................................................

Date: ..................................................... Score: ....................................

1.] $84\overline{)189}$

2.] $22\overline{)913}$

3.] $15\overline{)423}$

4.] $44\overline{)55}$

5.] $24\overline{)2142}$

6.] $88\overline{)990}$

# DIVISION

Name: ...................................................................................................

Date: ...................................................................... Score: ...........................

1.] 41$\overline{)328}$

2.] 31$\overline{)62}$

3.] 48$\overline{)1644}$

4.] 25$\overline{)1130}$

5.] 68$\overline{)425}$

6.] 39$\overline{)1794}$

Name: ...........................................................................................................

Date: ....................................................................... Score: ...................................

1.] $38\overline{)342}$

2.] $55\overline{)5236}$

3.] $12\overline{)78}$

4.] $24\overline{)150}$

5.] $21\overline{)105}$

6.] $62\overline{)3317}$

## DIVISION

Name: ................................................................................................

Date: ...............................................................  Score: ...........................

1.] $52\overline{)442}$  2.] $13\overline{)975}$  3.] $88\overline{)1254}$

4.] $22\overline{)913}$  5.] $68\overline{)3145}$  6.] $32\overline{)128}$

Name: ....................................................................................................

Date: ............................................................... Score: ...............................

1.] 35)‾1862‾

2.] 85)‾340‾

3.] 83)‾2739‾

4.] 55)‾2651‾

5.] 48)‾444‾

6.] 84)‾1785‾

Name: ...............................................................

Date: ...........................................................  Score: ...............................

1.] $84\overline{)588}$

2.] $48\overline{)2940}$

3.] $84\overline{)1449}$

4.] $88\overline{)374}$

5.] $35\overline{)77}$

6.] $22\overline{)363}$

Name: ................................................................

Date: ............................................... Score: ...........................

1.) $83\overline{)664}$

2.) $42\overline{)945}$

3.) $62\overline{)1302}$

4.) $59\overline{)295}$

5.) $44\overline{)363}$

6.) $75\overline{)3990}$

Name: .............................................................................................................

Date: .................................................................................    Score: ...............................

1.] $84\overline{)7665}$

2.] $88\overline{)616}$

3.] $32\overline{)1328}$

4.] $24\overline{)438}$

5.] $28\overline{)35}$

6.] $75\overline{)690}$

Name: ....................................................................................

Date: ....................................................... Score: ...........................

1.] $84\overline{)252}$

2.] $48\overline{)156}$

3.] $12\overline{)18}$

4.] $21\overline{)756}$

5.] $11\overline{)825}$

6.] $45\overline{)99}$

Name: ........................................................................................................

Date: ...................................................................... Score: .................................

1.] $25\overline{)130}$

2.] $38\overline{)342}$

3.] $47\overline{)658}$

4.] $44\overline{)143}$

5.] $55\overline{)2156}$

6.] $75\overline{)2190}$

Name: ........................................................................................................

Date: ......................................................... Score: ...............................

1.] $72\overline{)2052}$

2.] $24\overline{)1374}$

3.] $83\overline{)664}$

4.] $35\overline{)1722}$

5.] $73\overline{)2117}$

6.] $88\overline{)374}$

Name: .........................................................................................

Date: ..................................................... Score: .............................

1.] $74\overline{)148}$

2.] $35\overline{)287}$

3.] $42\overline{)231}$

4.] $48\overline{)204}$

5.] $84\overline{)777}$

6.] $25\overline{)2180}$

Name: ...............................................................................................................

Date: ...................................................................... Score: .......................................

---

**1.]** $32\overline{)752}$

**2.]** $15\overline{)63}$

**3.]** $52\overline{)1846}$

**4.]** $89\overline{)534}$

**5.]** $77\overline{)1771}$

**6.]** $42\overline{)63}$

# DIVISION

Name: ......................................................................................................

Date: ...................................................................... Score: ..................................

1.] $96\overline{)384}$

2.] $68\overline{)3689}$

3.] $93\overline{)2697}$

4.] $85\overline{)2227}$

5.] $69\overline{)1035}$

6.] $44\overline{)3575}$

Name: ..............................................................................................................

Date: .................................................................... Score: ..................................

1.] $68\overline{)425}$

2.] $48\overline{)108}$

3.] $45\overline{)4329}$

4.] $32\overline{)80}$

5.] $95\overline{)760}$

6.] $64\overline{)4816}$

Name: ............................................................................

Date: ....................................................................   Score: ...................................

1.] $28\overline{)35}$

2.] $35\overline{)287}$

3.] $92\overline{)1610}$

4.] $97\overline{)194}$

5.] $61\overline{)3477}$

6.] $24\overline{)1470}$

Name: .........................................................................................................

Date: .................................................. Score: ...............................

1.] $92\overline{)7314}$

2.] $85\overline{)4947}$

3.] $15\overline{)123}$

4.] $68\overline{)1649}$

5.] $88\overline{)550}$

6.] $22\overline{)77}$

Name: .................................................................................................

Date: ..................................................................  Score: ..................................

1.] $12\overline{)30}$

2.] $45\overline{)144}$

3.] $28\overline{)623}$

4.] $41\overline{)328}$

5.] $16\overline{)32}$

6.] $24\overline{)54}$

# Great Job Kid!

# Multiplication and division is Fun Right?
## Keep on learning!

# PROGRESS REPORT

| MULTILICATION | | DIVISION | |
|---|---|---|---|
| Exercise No | Score | Exercise No | Score |
| 1 | | 1 | |
| 2 | | 2 | |
| 3 | | 3 | |
| 4 | | 4 | |
| 5 | | 5 | |
| 6 | | 6 | |
| 7 | | 7 | |
| 8 | | 8 | |
| 9 | | 9 | |
| 10 | | 10 | |
| 11 | | 11 | |
| 12 | | 12 | |
| 13 | | 13 | |
| 14 | | 14 | |
| 15 | | 15 | |
| 16 | | 16 | |
| 17 | | 17 | |
| 18 | | 18 | |
| 19 | | 19 | |
| 20 | | 20 | |

# ANSWERS

# MULTIPLICATION EXERCISES

**Find the product.**

Name: ....................
Date: ....................        Score: ....................

1.)  90
   x 33
   2970

2.)  67
   x 57
   3819

3.)  48
   x 83
   3984

4.)  67
   x 70
   4690

5.)  79
   x 67
   5293

6.)  64
   x 76
   4864

7.)  16
   x 21
   336

8.)  63
   x 82
   5166

Name: ....................
Date: ....................        Score: ....................

1.)  89
   x 62
   5518

2.)  39
   x 59
   2301

3.)  66
   x 58
   3828

4.)  20
   x 45
   900

5.)  64
   x 91
   5824

6.)  32
   x 27
   864

7.)  12
   x 17
   204

8.)  73
   x 19
   1387

Name: ....................
Date: ....................        Score: ....................

1.)  98
   x 60
   5880

2.)  16
   x 56
   896

3.)  41
   x 37
   1517

4.)  10
   x 54
   540

5.)  34
   x 14
   476

6.)  16
   x 89
   1424

7.)  59
   x 34
   2006

8.)  36
   x 96
   3456

# MULTIPLICATION

## EXERCISE NO. 4

Name: ......................................................
Date: ....................................... Score: ...................

1.)
```
    24
  x 64
  1536
```

2.)
```
    44
  x 23
  1012
```

3.)
```
    25
  x 33
   825
```

4.)
```
    34
  x 45
  1530
```

5.)
```
    52
  x 31
  1612
```

6.)
```
    21
  x 66
  1386
```

7.)
```
    50
  x 83
  4150
```

8.)
```
    60
  x 79
  4740
```

# MULTIPLICATION

## EXERCISE NO. 5

Name: ......................................................
Date: ....................................... Score: ...................

1.)
```
    92
  x 61
  5612
```

2.)
```
    45
  x 58
  2610
```

3.)
```
    33
  x 61
  2013
```

4.)
```
    64
  x 70
  4480
```

5.)
```
    58
  x 64
  3712
```

6.)
```
    94
  x 12
  1128
```

7.)
```
    34
  x 88
  2992
```

8.)
```
    13
  x 80
  1040
```

# MULTIPLICATION

## EXERCISE NO. 6

Name: ......................................................
Date: ....................................... Score: ...................

1.)
```
    13
  x 48
   624
```

2.)
```
    54
  x 76
  4104
```

3.)
```
    80
  x 30
  2400
```

4.)
```
    11
  x 24
   264
```

5.)
```
    76
  x 32
  2432
```

6.)
```
    57
  x 20
  1140
```

7.)
```
    41
  x 75
  3075
```

8.)
```
    66
  x 60
  3960
```

# MULTIPLICATION

## EXERCISE NO. 7

Name: ......................................................
Date: ....................................... Score: ...................

1.)
```
    69
  x 24
  1656
```

2.)
```
    88
  x 54
  4752
```

3.)
```
    56
  x 98
  5488
```

4.)
```
    91
  x 16
  1456
```

5.)
```
    39
  x 60
  2340
```

6.)
```
    16
  x 86
  1376
```

7.)
```
    40
  x 68
  2720
```

8.)
```
    40
  x 89
  3560
```

## MULTIPLICATION

### EXERCISE NO. 8

Name:
Date:                                    Score:

1.)
```
    96
  x 76
  7296
```
2.)
```
    78
  x 20
  1560
```
3.)
```
    38
  x 36
  1368
```
4.)
```
    15
  x 71
  1065
```

5.)
```
    35
  x 84
  2940
```
6.)
```
    35
  x 12
   420
```
7.)
```
    33
  x 19
   627
```
8.)
```
    27
  x 35
   945
```

## MULTIPLICATION

### EXERCISE NO. 9

Name:
Date:                                    Score:

1.)
```
    59
  x 70
  4130
```
2.)
```
    21
  x 77
  1617
```
3.)
```
    95
  x 92
  8740
```
4.)
```
    33
  x 78
  2574
```

5.)
```
    25
  x 52
  1300
```
6.)
```
    33
  x 56
  1848
```
7.)
```
    83
  x 19
  1577
```
8.)
```
    73
  x 13
   949
```

## MULTIPLICATION

### EXERCISE NO. 10

Name:
Date:                                    Score:

1.)
```
    42
  x 17
   714
```
2.)
```
    72
  x 57
  4104
```
3.)
```
    37
  x 47
  1739
```
4.)
```
    62
  x 27
  1674
```

5.)
```
    38
  x 28
  1064
```
6.)
```
    67
  x 41
  2747
```
7.)
```
    24
  x 36
   864
```
8.)
```
    72
  x 48
  3456
```

## MULTIPLICATION

### EXERCISE NO. 11

Name:
Date:                                    Score:

1.)
```
    18
  x 19
   342
```
2.)
```
    50
  x 25
  1250
```
3.)
```
    27
  x 12
   324
```
4.)
```
    66
  x 44
  2904
```

5.)
```
    61
  x 21
  1281
```
6.)
```
    87
  x 11
   957
```
7.)
```
    22
  x 22
   484
```
8.)
```
    84
  x 33
  2772
```

## MULTIPLICATION

### EXERCISE NO. 12

Name: ...............................................
Date: ...............................     Score: ....................

1.)  91
  x 95
  8645

2.)  16
  x 73
  1168

3.)  95
  x 40
  3800

4.)  52
  x 50
  2600

5.)  27
  x 21
  567

6.)  45
  x 84
  3780

7.)  28
  x 53
  1484

8.)  56
  x 10
  560

## MULTIPLICATION

### EXERCISE NO. 13

Name: ...............................................
Date: ...............................     Score: ....................

1.)  10
  x 40
  400

2.)  86
  x 38
  3268

3.)  83
  x 25
  2075

4.)  33
  x 40
  1320

5.)  44
  x 31
  1364

6.)  24
  x 85
  2040

7.)  64
  x 47
  3008

8.)  46
  x 65
  2990

## MULTIPLICATION

### EXERCISE NO. 14

Name: ...............................................
Date: ...............................     Score: ....................

1.)  88
  x 79
  6952

2.)  80
  x 40
  3200

3.)  15
  x 47
  705

4.)  78
  x 54
  4212

5.)  78
  x 62
  4836

6.)  61
  x 33
  2013

7.)  33
  x 46
  1518

8.)  72
  x 15
  1080

## MULTIPLICATION

### EXERCISE NO. 15

Name: ...............................................
Date: ...............................     Score: ....................

1.)  21
  x 40
  840

2.)  66
  x 89
  5874

3.)  56
  x 14
  784

4.)  11
  x 92
  1012

5.)  23
  x 16
  368

6.)  17
  x 62
  1054

7.)  19
  x 31
  589

8.)  82
  x 88
  7216

## MULTIPLICATION — EXERCISE NO. 16

Name: ................
Date: ................                Score: ................

1.)  50
   x 28
   ────
   1400

2.)  47
   x 77
   ────
   3619

3.)  93
   x 65
   ────
   6045

4.)  34
   x 75
   ────
   2550

5.)  99
   x 53
   ────
   5247

6.)  55
   x 63
   ────
   3465

7.)  58
   x 71
   ────
   4118

8.)  53
   x 79
   ────
   4187

## MULTIPLICATION — EXERCISE NO. 18

Name: ................
Date: ................                Score: ................

1.)  50
   x 28
   ────
   1400

2.)  47
   x 77
   ────
   3619

3.)  93
   x 65
   ────
   6045

4.)  34
   x 75
   ────
   2550

5.)  99
   x 53
   ────
   5247

6.)  55
   x 63
   ────
   3465

7.)  58
   x 71
   ────
   4118

8.)  53
   x 79
   ────
   4187

## MULTIPLICATION — EXERCISE NO. 17

Name: ................
Date: ................                Score: ................

1.)  21
   x 40
   ────
   840

2.)  66
   x 89
   ────
   5874

3.)  56
   x 14
   ────
   784

4.)  11
   x 92
   ────
   1012

5.)  23
   x 16
   ────
   368

6.)  17
   x 62
   ────
   1054

7.)  19
   x 31
   ────
   589

8.)  82
   x 88
   ────
   7216

## MULTIPLICATION — EXERCISE NO. 19

Name: ................
Date: ................                Score: ................

1.)  48
   x 29
   ────
   1392

2.)  25
   x 43
   ────
   1075

3.)  89
   x 13
   ────
   1157

4.)  59
   x 71
   ────
   4189

5.)  11
   x 21
   ────
   231

6.)  83
   x 85
   ────
   7055

7.)  42
   x 96
   ────
   4032

8.)  66
   x 10
   ────
   660

Name: ....................

Date: ....................   Score: ....................

1.)  42
    x 50
    ─────
    2100

2.)  91
    x 90
    ─────
    8190

3.)  89
    x 75
    ─────
    6675

4.)  24
    x 91
    ─────
    2184

5.)  81
    x 26
    ─────
    2106

6.)  25
    x 88
    ─────
    2200

7.)  21
    x 88
    ─────
    1848

8.)  18
    x 93
    ─────
    1674

# DIVISION EXERCISES

**Find the quotient.**

Name: ....................

Date: ....................   Score: ....................

1.) 24)144̄ = 6

2.) 72)396.0̄ = 5.5

3.) 46)1886̄ = 41

4.) 48)4668.00̄ = 97.25

5.) 12)78.0̄ = 6.5

6.) 42)693.0̄ = 16.5

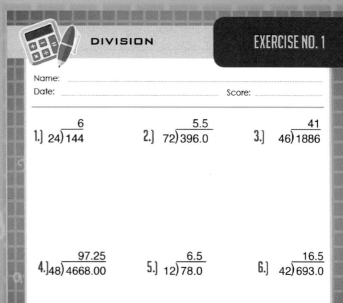

## DIVISION — EXERCISE NO. 2

Name: ........................................................

Date: ....................................... Score: .......................

1.] $\dfrac{6}{21 \overline{)126}}$  2.] $\dfrac{55.25}{24 \overline{)1326.00}}$  3.] $\dfrac{34}{47 \overline{)1598}}$

4.] $\dfrac{98}{35 \overline{)3430}}$  5.] $\dfrac{2}{13 \overline{)26}}$  6.] $\dfrac{38.}{45 \overline{)1719.}}$

## DIVISION — EXERCISE NO. 3

Name: ........................................................

Date: ....................................... Score: .......................

1.] $\dfrac{1.5}{32 \overline{)48.0}}$  2.] $\dfrac{35.2}{15 \overline{)528.0}}$  3.] $\dfrac{4.2}{64 \overline{)272.0}}$

4.] $\dfrac{78.25}{68 \overline{)5321.00}}$  5.] $\dfrac{42}{37 \overline{)1554}}$  6.] $\dfrac{96}{42 \overline{)4032}}$

## DIVISION — EXERCISE NO. 4

Name: ........................................................

Date: ....................................... Score: .......................

1.] $\dfrac{2.25}{84 \overline{)189.00}}$  2.] $\dfrac{41.5}{22 \overline{)913.0}}$  3.] $\dfrac{28.2}{15 \overline{)423.0}}$

4.] $\dfrac{1.25}{44 \overline{)55.00}}$  5.] $\dfrac{89.25}{24 \overline{)2142.00}}$  6.] $\dfrac{11.2}{88 \overline{)990.0}}$

## DIVISION — EXERCISE NO. 5

Name: ........................................................

Date: ....................................... Score: .......................

1.] $\dfrac{8}{41 \overline{)328}}$  2.] $\dfrac{2}{31 \overline{)62}}$  3.] $\dfrac{34.}{48 \overline{)1644.}}$

4.] $\dfrac{45.2}{25 \overline{)1130.0}}$  5.] $\dfrac{6.25}{68 \overline{)425.00}}$  6.] $\dfrac{46}{39 \overline{)1794}}$

## DIVISION

**EXERCISE NO. 6**

Name: ................................................

Date: ...................................... Score: ......................

1.)  9  
38) 342

2.)  95.2  
55) 5236.0

3.)  6.5  
12) 78.0

4.)  6.25  
24) 150.00

5.)  5  
21) 105

6.)  53.  
62) 3317.

## DIVISION

**EXERCISE NO. 7**

Name: ................................................

Date: ...................................... Score: ......................

1.)  8.5  
52) 442.0

2.)  75  
13) 975

3.)  14.  
88) 1254.

4.)  41.5  
22) 913.0

5.)  46.25  
68) 3145.00

6.)  4  
32) 128

## DIVISION

**EXERCISE NO. 8**

Name: ................................................

Date: ...................................... Score: ......................

1.)  53.2  
35) 1862.0

2.)  4  
85) 340

3.)  33  
83) 2739

4.)  48.2  
55) 2651.0

5.)  9.25  
48) 444.00

6.)  21.  
84) 1785.

## DIVISION

**EXERCISE NO. 9**

Name: ................................................

Date: ...................................... Score: ......................

1.)  7  
84) 588

2.)  61.25  
48) 2940.00

3.)  17.  
84) 1449.

4.)  4.25  
88) 374.00

5.)  2.2  
35) 77.0

6.)  16.5  
22) 363.0

## DIVISION — EXERCISE NO. 10

Name: ..................................................
Date: .......................................... Score: ..........................

1.] $\frac{8}{83\,)\,664}$

2.] $\frac{22.5}{42\,)\,945.0}$

3.] $\frac{21}{62\,)\,1302}$

4.] $\frac{5}{59\,)\,295}$

5.] $\frac{8.25}{44\,)\,363.00}$

6.] $\frac{53.}{75\,)\,3990.}$

## DIVISION — EXERCISE NO. 11

Name: ..................................................
Date: .......................................... Score: ..........................

1.] $\frac{91.25}{84\,)\,7665.00}$

2.] $\frac{7}{88\,)\,616}$

3.] $\frac{41.}{32\,)\,1328.}$

4.] $\frac{18.25}{24\,)\,438.00}$

5.] $\frac{1.25}{28\,)\,35.00}$

6.] $\frac{9.2}{75\,)\,690.0}$

## DIVISION — EXERCISE NO. 12

Name: ..................................................
Date: .......................................... Score: ..........................

1.] $\frac{3}{84\,)\,252}$

2.] $\frac{3.25}{48\,)\,156.00}$

3.] $\frac{1.5}{12\,)\,18.0}$

4.] $\frac{36}{21\,)\,756}$

5.] $\frac{75}{11\,)\,825}$

6.] $\frac{2.2}{45\,)\,99.0}$

## DIVISION — EXERCISE NO. 13

Name: ..................................................
Date: .......................................... Score: ..........................

1.] $\frac{5.2}{25\,)\,130.0}$

2.] $\frac{9}{38\,)\,342}$

3.] $\frac{14}{47\,)\,658}$

4.] $\frac{3.25}{44\,)\,143.00}$

5.] $\frac{39.2}{55\,)\,2156.0}$

6.] $\frac{29.}{75\,)\,2190.}$

Name: ....................................

Date: ....................................  Score: ....................................

1.] $72\overline{)2052.0}$ = 28.5

2.] $24\overline{)1374.00}$ = 57.25

3.] $83\overline{)664}$ = 8

4.] $35\overline{)1722.0}$ = 49.2

5.] $73\overline{)2117}$ = 29

6.] $88\overline{)374.0}$ = 4.2

Name: ....................................

Date: ....................................  Score: ....................................

1.] $74\overline{)148}$ = 2

2.] $35\overline{)287.0}$ = 8.2

3.] $42\overline{)231.0}$ = 5.5

4.] $48\overline{)204.00}$ = 4.25

5.] $84\overline{)777.00}$ = 9.25

6.] $25\overline{)2180.}$ = 87.

Name: ....................................

Date: ....................................  Score: ....................................

1.] $32\overline{)752.0}$ = 23.5

2.] $15\overline{)63.0}$ = 4.2

3.] $52\overline{)1846.}$ = 35.

4.] $89\overline{)534}$ = 6

5.] $77\overline{)1771}$ = 23

6.] $42\overline{)63.0}$ = 1.5

Name: ....................................

Date: ....................................  Score: ....................................

1.] $96\overline{)384}$ = 4

2.] $68\overline{)3689.00}$ = 54.25

3.] $93\overline{)2697}$ = 29

4.] $85\overline{)2227.0}$ = 26.2

5.] $69\overline{)1035}$ = 15

6.] $44\overline{)3575.}$ = 81.

Name: ......................................................
Date: ........................................ Score: ..................

1.]  6.25 / 68) 425.00

2.]  2.25 / 48) 108.00

3.]  96. / 45) 4329.

4.]  2.5 / 32) 80.0

5.]  8 / 95) 760

6.]  75. / 64) 4816.

Name: ......................................................
Date: ........................................ Score: ..................

1.]  1.25 / 28) 35.00

2.]  8.2 / 35) 287.0

3.]  17. / 92) 1610.

4.]  2 / 97) 194

5.]  57 / 61) 3477

6.]  61. / 24) 1470.

Name: ......................................................
Date: ........................................ Score: ..................

1.]  79.5 / 92) 7314.0

2.]  58.2 / 85) 4947.0

3.]  8.2 / 15) 123.0

4.]  24.25 / 68) 1649.00

5.]  6.25 / 88) 550.00

6.]  3.5 / 22) 77.0

Name: ......................................................
Date: ........................................ Score: ..................

1.]  2.5 / 12) 30.0

2.]  3.2 / 45) 144.0

3.]  22.2 / 28) 623.0

4.]  8 / 41) 328

5.]  2 / 16) 32

6.]  2.25 / 24) 54.00

Made in the USA
Las Vegas, NV
28 September 2021